THIS JOURNAL

Belongs To:

_____

Dedication

This Camping Journal Log book is dedicated to all the people out there who love to go camping and document their findings in the process.

You are my inspiration for producing books and I'm honored to be a part of keeping all of your Camping notes and records organized.

This journal notebook will help you record your details about your camping adventures.

Thoughtfully put together with these sections to record:

Camping Calendar, Camping Tracker, Camping Reservation, Campground Amenities, Camping Shopping List, Family Camping Checklist, Camping Supplies, Meal Planner, Camping Journal Pages, Fishing, Hiking, and much more!

How to Use this Book

The purpose of this book is to keep all of your Camping notes all in one place. It will help keep you organized.

This Camping Journal will allow you to accurately document every detail about your camping trips. It's a great way to chart your course through your camping adventures.

Here are examples of the prompts for you to fill in and write about your experience in this book:

1. **Contact Page** - Write your name.

2. **Camping Calendar** - Undated, color in the dates you went camping.

3. **Camping Tracker** - Track Where You've Been (Campsite, Site Location, Date)

4. **Camping Reservation** - Address, Phone Number, Reservation Details, Food, Activities.

5. **Campground Amenities** - Check boxes for water, electricity, sewer, wifi, showers, swimming, fishing, etc.

6. **Camping Shopping List** - Make your list of things you need to buy for the trip.

7. **Family Camping Checklist** - Detailed check boxes for Important Gear, Food Supplies, Clothing, Tools & Supplies, Misc Items & Other.

8. **Camping Supplies** - Your own personal list of things you need to pack.

9. **Camping Checklist** - Shelter, Food, Essentials, Comfort, Clothing, Personal, Important, Entertainment, Cleaning, Misc.

10. **Meal Planner** - Space for writing your meals for each day of the week plus snacks.

11. **Activity** - Write the activities you participated in for each day of the week, the fun things you did.

12. **Camping Journal Pages** - Date, What You Did Today, Highlights Of The Day, Favorite Memory On The Road.

13. **Fishing Expedition** - Keep Track Of The Fish You Catch, Lake/ Area, Type Of Fish, Weight.

14. **Hiking Checklist** - Detailed check boxes for Clothing, Equipment, Food & Supplies, Camping Gear, Misc, Other.

15. **Hiking Journal** - Record the information & details of your hike. Trail, Location, Elevation Gain/ Loss, Distance, Duration, Trail Type, Difficulty, Start/ End Time, Weather, Blank Lined Notes.

CAMPING *Adventures*

COLOR IN THE DATES WHEN YOU WENT CAMPING

JANUARY

S	M	T	W	T	F	S

FEBRUARY

S	M	T	W	T	F	S

MARCH

S	M	T	W	T	F	S

APRIL

S	M	T	W	T	F	S

MAY

S	M	T	W	T	F	S

JUNE

S	M	T	W	T	F	S

JULY

S	M	T	W	T	F	S

AUGUST

S	M	T	W	T	F	S

SEPTEMBER

S	M	T	W	T	F	S

OCTOBER

S	M	T	W	T	F	S

NOVEMBER

S	M	T	W	T	F	S

DECEMBER

S	M	T	W	T	F	S

CAMPING TRACKER
Where I've Been

CAMPGROUND	LOCATION	DATE

CAMPING RESERVATION

CAMPGROUND PHONE #	RESERVATION DETAILS
CONTACT PERSON	
CAMPGROUND ADDRESS	**ACTIVITIES**
RESTAURANTS & AMENITIES	**NOTES**

SITE #	NIGHTLY RATE	CHECK IN	CHECK OUT

CAMPGROUND
Amenities

- WATER
- ELECTRIC
- SEWER
- WIFI
- CABLE TV
- PETS ALLOWED
- FIRE PIT
- SHOWERS
- TENTS PERMITTED
- VISITOR PARKING
- LAUNDRY SERVICES
- BBQ AREA
- SWIMMING
- ACCESS TO BEACH / LAKE
- BOAT LAUNCH
- FISHING

- POOL
- HOT TUB
- ACTIVITY CENTER
- NATURE TRAILS / HIKING
- PLAYGROUND
- BIKING / TRAILS
- GOLF COURSE
- KIDS CENTER
- FIREWORKS
- BINGO
- VOLLEYBALL
- TENNIS COURTS
- GARBAGE DISPOSAL
- CONVENIENCE STORE
- FIREWOOD/KINDLE
- PICNIC TABLES

CAMPING *Shopping List*

FAMILY CAMPING
Checklist

IMPORTANT GEAR

- ☐ Tent
- ☐ Backpack
- ☐ Tarp
- ☐ BBQ
- ☐ Sleeping Bag
- ☐ Camping Chairs
- ☐ _____
- ☐ _____
- ☐ _____
- ☐ _____
- ☐ _____

FOOD SUPPLIES

- ☐ Meals
- ☐ Snacks
- ☐ Water & Drinks
- ☐ Cook Set / Pots &
- ☐ Utensils & Dishes
- ☐ Condiments
- ☐ _____
- ☐ _____
- ☐ _____
- ☐ _____
- ☐ _____

CLOTHING

- ☐ Gloves & Hat
- ☐ Hats / Visors
- ☐ Socks & Underwear
- ☐ T-shirts & Sweaters
- ☐ Jacket / Raincoat
- ☐ Hiking Boots
- ☐ _____
- ☐ _____
- ☐ _____
- ☐ _____
- ☐ _____

TOOLS & SUPPLIES

- ☐ Lighter & Flashlights
- ☐ Firewood & Fire Starter
- ☐ Batteries
- ☐ Knife or Multi-Tool
- ☐ Compass
- ☐ _____
- ☐ _____
- ☐ _____
- ☐ _____
- ☐ _____

MISC ITEMS

- ☐ Garbage Bags
- ☐ Sunscreen
- ☐ Bug Spray/ Repellent
- ☐ Towels
- ☐ Water Bottle
- ☐ Toilet Paper
- ☐ _____
- ☐ _____
- ☐ _____
- ☐ _____

OTHER

- ☐ _____
- ☐ _____
- ☐ _____
- ☐ _____
- ☐ _____
- ☐ _____
- ☐ _____
- ☐ _____
- ☐ _____

FAMILY CAMPING

Checklist

IMPORTANT GEAR

- ☐ _____
- ☐ _____
- ☐ _____
- ☐ _____
- ☐ _____
- ☐ _____
- ☐ _____
- ☐ _____
- ☐ _____
- ☐ _____

FOOD SUPPLIES

- ☐ _____
- ☐ _____
- ☐ _____
- ☐ _____
- ☐ _____
- ☐ _____
- ☐ _____
- ☐ _____
- ☐ _____
- ☐ _____

CLOTHING

- ☐ _____
- ☐ _____
- ☐ _____
- ☐ _____
- ☐ _____
- ☐ _____
- ☐ _____
- ☐ _____
- ☐ _____
- ☐ _____

TOOLS & SUPPLIES

- ☐ _____
- ☐ _____
- ☐ _____
- ☐ _____
- ☐ _____
- ☐ _____
- ☐ _____
- ☐ _____
- ☐ _____
- ☐ _____

MISC ITEMS

- ☐ _____
- ☐ _____
- ☐ _____
- ☐ _____
- ☐ _____
- ☐ _____
- ☐ _____
- ☐ _____
- ☐ _____
- ☐ _____

OTHER

- ☐ _____
- ☐ _____
- ☐ _____
- ☐ _____
- ☐ _____
- ☐ _____
- ☐ _____
- ☐ _____
- ☐ _____
- ☐ _____

CAMPING SUPPLIES

- [ ] _____
- [ ] _____
- [ ] _____
- [ ] _____
- [ ] _____
- [ ] _____
- [ ] _____
- [ ] _____
- [ ] _____
- [ ] _____
- [ ] _____
- [ ] _____
- [ ] _____
- [ ] _____
- [ ] _____
- [ ] _____
- [ ] _____
- [ ] _____
- [ ] _____
- [ ] _____
- [ ] _____
- [ ] _____

- [ ] _____
- [ ] _____
- [ ] _____
- [ ] _____
- [ ] _____
- [ ] _____
- [ ] _____
- [ ] _____
- [ ] _____
- [ ] _____
- [ ] _____
- [ ] _____
- [ ] _____
- [ ] _____
- [ ] _____
- [ ] _____
- [ ] _____
- [ ] _____
- [ ] _____
- [ ] _____
- [ ] _____
- [ ] _____

- [ ] _____
- [ ] _____
- [ ] _____
- [ ] _____
- [ ] _____
- [ ] _____
- [ ] _____
- [ ] _____
- [ ] _____
- [ ] _____
- [ ] _____
- [ ] _____
- [ ] _____
- [ ] _____
- [ ] _____
- [ ] _____
- [ ] _____
- [ ] _____
- [ ] _____
- [ ] _____
- [ ] _____
- [ ] _____

CAMPING *Checklist*

Shelter

- [ ] TENT / CAMPER
- [ ] SLEEPING BLANKET
- [ ] PILLOWS
- [ ] TARP / COVERING

Comport

- [ ] SLEEPING BAGS
- [ ] SHEETS & PILLOWS
- [ ] AIR MATTRESS
- [ ] AIR PUMP

- [ ] HIKING BOOTS
- [ ] SWEATERS
- [ ] RAIN JACKET
- [ ] WARM SOCKS
- [ ] T-SHIRTS
- [ ] WARM COAT
- [ ] SUN VISOR / HAT
- [ ] BATHING SUIT
- [ ] PYJAMAS

Food

- [ ] FOOD / SUPPLIES
- [ ] CONDIMENTS
- [ ] COOKWARE/POTS
- [ ] TABLE CLOTH
- [ ] PLATES & CUPS
- [ ] UTENSILS
- [ ] PAPER TOWEL
- [ ] POT HOLDERS
- [ ] DISH SOAP
- [ ] CUTLERY

Personal

- [ ] SOAP
- [ ] SHAMPOO
- [ ] TOWELS
- [ ] TOOTHPASTE
- [ ] HAIR BRUSH
- [ ] SUNSCREEN
- [ ] DEODORANT
- [ ] HAND SANITIZER
- [ ] RAZORS

Essentials

- [ ] MEDICATION
- [ ] FIRST AID KIT
- [ ] TOILET PAPER
- [ ] LIP BALM
- [ ] TISSUES
- [ ] MIRROR
- [ ] HAIR CLIPS

Important

- [ ] BATTERIES
- [ ] CAMERA
- [ ] CHARGERS
- [ ] SUNGLASSES
- [ ] FLASHLIGHT
- [ ] BUG SPRAY
- [ ] LANTERNS
- [ ] COMPASS
- [ ] BINOCULARS
- [ ] HIKING GEAR
- [ ] BACKPACK

CAMPING *Checklist*

Entertainment

- [ ] BOARD GAMES
- [ ] CARDS
- [ ] RADIO
- [ ] SPORTS GEAR

Cleaning

- [ ] BROOM / MOP
- [ ] CLEANING SUPPLIES
- [ ] CLEANING CLOTHS
- [ ] DISH TOWELS

Misc

- [ ] COFFEE POT
- [ ] FIRE KETTLE
- [ ] COOLER & ICE
- [ ] FOLDABLE TABLE
- [ ] CAMPING CHAIRS
- [ ] LIGHTER / FUEL
- [ ] FIREWOOD
- [ ] BBQ GRLL
- [ ] GARBAGE BAGS

Shopping List

CAMPING MEAL *Planner*

MONDAY

TUESDAY

WEDNESDAY

THURSDAY

FRIDAY

SATURDAY

SUNDAY

SNACK IDEAS

CAMPING *Activities*

Monday

Tuesday

Wednesday

Thursday

Friday

Saturday

Sunday

MY CAMPING *Journal*

DATE:

WHAT I DID TODAY

HIGHLIGHT OF THE DAY

CAMPING *Memories*

DATE & CAMPSITE

WHAT WE DID

HIGHLIGHT OF THE TRIP

FISHING EXPEDITION
What I've Caught

LAKE / AREA	TYPE OF FISH	WEIGHT

FAMILY CAMPING
Adventures

CAMPGROUND

DATE

ACTIVITIES

HIGHLIGHT OF THE TRIP

FAVORITE MEMORY

HIKING CHECKLIST

CLOTHING

- ☐ HIKING BOOTS
- ☐ WOOL SOCKS
- ☐ BASE LAYERS
- ☐ SHORT SLEEVED SHIRT
- ☐ LONG SLEEVED SHIRT
- ☐ INSULATED MIDLAYER
- ☐ SUN HAT / VISOR
- ☐ BANDANA
- ☐ RAINWEAR
- ☐ WATCH

EQUIPMENT

- ☐ MAP
- ☐ COMPASS
- ☐ FLASHLIGHT
- ☐ HEAD LAMP
- ☐ LIGHTER / MATCHES
- ☐ KNIFE / MULTI-TOOL
- ☐ CELL PHONE
- ☐ POUCH
- ☐ MOLESKIN
- ☐ TREKKING POLES

FOOD & SUPPLIES

- ☐ MEALS & SNACKS
- ☐ WATER BOTTLE
- ☐ WATER TREATMENT
- ☐ COOKING POT
- ☐ COOKSTOVE/FUEL
- ☐ EATING UTENSILS
- ☐ BOWL/MUG/PLATE
- ☐ GARBAGE BAGS
- ☐ ROPE
- ☐ FOLDABLE BUCKET

CAMPING GEAR

- ☐ TENT
- ☐ SLEEPING BAG
- ☐ SLEEPING PAD
- ☐ TOILET PAPER
- ☐ BACKPACK
- ☐ DUCT TAPE
- ☐ FOLDING SAW
- ☐ POT LIFTER
- ☐ CAMP SHOES
- ☐ BEAR BANGER

MISC.

- ☐ INSECT REPELLENT
- ☐ LIP BALM
- ☐ FACE PROTECTOR
- ☐ EXTRA GLOVES
- ☐ DEODORANT
- ☐ HEADPHONES
- ☐ BATTERIES
- ☐ CHARGER
- ☐ DECK OF CARDS
- ☐ GPS

OTHER

- ☐ _____
- ☐ _____
- ☐ _____
- ☐ _____
- ☐ _____
- ☐ _____
- ☐ _____
- ☐ _____
- ☐ _____
- ☐ _____

HIKING JOURNAL

TRAIL	ELEVATION GAIN	LOSS
LOCATION		

DISTANCE	DURATION	START TIME	END TIME

TRAIL TYPE	DIFFICULTY	WEATHER

IMPORTANT TRAIL DETAILS	NOTES

TRAIL SURFACE	EXPOSURE	

CAMPING *Adventures*

COLOR IN THE DATES WHEN YOU WENT CAMPING

JANUARY						
S	M	T	W	T	F	S

FEBRUARY						
S	M	T	W	T	F	S

MARCH						
S	M	T	W	T	F	S

APRIL						
S	M	T	W	T	F	S

MAY						
S	M	T	W	T	F	S

JUNE						
S	M	T	W	T	F	S

JULY						
S	M	T	W	T	F	S

AUGUST						
S	M	T	W	T	F	S

SEPTEMBER						
S	M	T	W	T	F	S

OCTOBER						
S	M	T	W	T	F	S

NOVEMBER						
S	M	T	W	T	F	S

DECEMBER						
S	M	T	W	T	F	S

CAMPING TRACKER
Where I've Been

	CAMPGROUND	LOCATION	DATE

CAMPING RESERVATION

CAMPGROUND PHONE #	RESERVATION DETAILS
CONTACT PERSON	
CAMPGROUND ADDRESS	ACTIVITIES
RESTAURANTS & AMENITIES	NOTES

SITE #	NIGHTLY RATE	CHECK IN	CHECK OUT

CAMPGROUND
Amenities

- WATER
- ELECTRIC
- SEWER
- WIFI
- CABLE TV
- PETS ALLOWED
- FIRE PIT
- SHOWERS
- TENTS PERMITTED
- VISITOR PARKING
- LAUNDRY SERVICES
- BBQ AREA
- SWIMMING
- ACCESS TO BEACH / LAKE
- BOAT LAUNCH
- FISHING

- POOL
- HOT TUB
- ACTIVITY CENTER
- NATURE TRAILS / HIKING
- PLAYGROUND
- BIKING / TRAILS
- GOLF COURSE
- KIDS CENTER
- FIREWORKS
- BINGO
- VOLLEYBALL
- TENNIS COURTS
- GARBAGE DISPOSAL
- CONVENIENCE STORE
- FIREWOOD/KINDLE
- PICNIC TABLES

CAMPING *Shopping List*

FAMILY CAMPING
Checklist

IMPORTANT GEAR

- ☐ Tent
- ☐ Backpack
- ☐ Tarp
- ☐ BBQ
- ☐ Sleeping Bag
- ☐ Camping Chairs
- ☐ _____
- ☐ _____
- ☐ _____
- ☐ _____
- ☐ _____

FOOD SUPPLIES

- ☐ Meals
- ☐ Snacks
- ☐ Water & Drinks
- ☐ Cook Set / Pots &
- ☐ Utensils & Dishes
- ☐ Condiments
- ☐ _____
- ☐ _____
- ☐ _____
- ☐ _____
- ☐ _____

CLOTHING

- ☐ Gloves & Hat
- ☐ Hats / Visors
- ☐ Socks & Underwear
- ☐ T-shirts & Sweaters
- ☐ Jacket / Raincoat
- ☐ Hiking Boots
- ☐ _____
- ☐ _____
- ☐ _____
- ☐ _____
- ☐ _____

TOOLS & SUPPLIES

- ☐ Lighter & Flashlights
- ☐ Firewood & Fire Starter
- ☐ Batteries
- ☐ Knife or Multi-Tool
- ☐ Compass
- ☐ _____
- ☐ _____
- ☐ _____
- ☐ _____
- ☐ _____

MISC ITEMS

- ☐ Garbage Bags
- ☐ Sunscreen
- ☐ Bug Spray/ Repellent
- ☐ Towels
- ☐ Water Bottle
- ☐ Toilet Paper
- ☐ _____
- ☐ _____
- ☐ _____
- ☐ _____

OTHER

- ☐ _____
- ☐ _____
- ☐ _____
- ☐ _____
- ☐ _____
- ☐ _____
- ☐ _____
- ☐ _____
- ☐ _____
- ☐ _____

FAMILY CAMPING

Checklist

IMPORTANT GEAR

- ☐ _____
- ☐ _____
- ☐ _____
- ☐ _____
- ☐ _____
- ☐ _____
- ☐ _____
- ☐ _____
- ☐ _____
- ☐ _____

FOOD SUPPLIES

- ☐ _____
- ☐ _____
- ☐ _____
- ☐ _____
- ☐ _____
- ☐ _____
- ☐ _____
- ☐ _____
- ☐ _____
- ☐ _____

CLOTHING

- ☐ _____
- ☐ _____
- ☐ _____
- ☐ _____
- ☐ _____
- ☐ _____
- ☐ _____
- ☐ _____
- ☐ _____
- ☐ _____

TOOLS & SUPPLIES

- ☐ _____
- ☐ _____
- ☐ _____
- ☐ _____
- ☐ _____
- ☐ _____
- ☐ _____
- ☐ _____
- ☐ _____
- ☐ _____

MISC ITEMS

- ☐ _____
- ☐ _____
- ☐ _____
- ☐ _____
- ☐ _____
- ☐ _____
- ☐ _____
- ☐ _____
- ☐ _____
- ☐ _____

OTHER

- ☐ _____
- ☐ _____
- ☐ _____
- ☐ _____
- ☐ _____
- ☐ _____
- ☐ _____
- ☐ _____
- ☐ _____
- ☐ _____

CAMPING SUPPLIES

- ☐ _____
- ☐ _____
- ☐ _____
- ☐ _____
- ☐ _____
- ☐ _____
- ☐ _____
- ☐ _____
- ☐ _____
- ☐ _____
- ☐ _____
- ☐ _____
- ☐ _____
- ☐ _____
- ☐ _____
- ☐ _____
- ☐ _____
- ☐ _____
- ☐ _____
- ☐ _____
- ☐ _____
- ☐ _____

- ☐ _____
- ☐ _____
- ☐ _____
- ☐ _____
- ☐ _____
- ☐ _____
- ☐ _____
- ☐ _____
- ☐ _____
- ☐ _____
- ☐ _____
- ☐ _____
- ☐ _____
- ☐ _____
- ☐ _____
- ☐ _____
- ☐ _____
- ☐ _____
- ☐ _____
- ☐ _____
- ☐ _____
- ☐ _____

- ☐ _____
- ☐ _____
- ☐ _____
- ☐ _____
- ☐ _____
- ☐ _____
- ☐ _____
- ☐ _____
- ☐ _____
- ☐ _____
- ☐ _____
- ☐ _____
- ☐ _____
- ☐ _____
- ☐ _____
- ☐ _____
- ☐ _____
- ☐ _____
- ☐ _____
- ☐ _____
- ☐ _____
- ☐ _____

CAMPING *Checklist*

Shelter

- [ ] TENT / CAMPER
- [ ] SLEEPING BLANKET
- [ ] PILLOWS
- [ ] TARP / COVERING

Comport

- [ ] SLEEPING BAGS
- [ ] SHEETS & PILLOWS
- [ ] AIR MATTRESS
- [ ] AIR PUMP

- [ ] HIKING BOOTS
- [ ] SWEATERS
- [ ] RAIN JACKET
- [ ] WARM SOCKS
- [ ] T-SHIRTS
- [ ] WARM COAT
- [ ] SUN VISOR / HAT
- [ ] BATHING SUIT
- [ ] PYJAMAS

Food

- [ ] FOOD / SUPPLIES
- [ ] CONDIMENTS
- [ ] COOKWARE/POTS
- [ ] TABLE CLOTH
- [ ] PLATES & CUPS
- [ ] UTENSILS
- [ ] PAPER TOWEL
- [ ] POT HOLDERS
- [ ] DISH SOAP
- [ ] CUTLERY

Personal

- [ ] SOAP
- [ ] SHAMPOO
- [ ] TOWELS
- [ ] TOOTHPASTE
- [ ] HAIR BRUSH
- [ ] SUNSCREEN
- [ ] DEODORANT
- [ ] HAND SANITIZER
- [ ] RAZORS

Essentials

- [ ] MEDICATION
- [ ] FIRST AID KIT
- [ ] TOILET PAPER
- [ ] LIP BALM
- [ ] TISSUES
- [ ] MIRROR
- [ ] HAIR CLIPS

Important

- [ ] BATTERIES
- [ ] CAMERA
- [ ] CHARGERS
- [ ] SUNGLASSES
- [ ] FLASHLIGHT
- [ ] BUG SPRAY
- [ ] LANTERNS
- [ ] COMPASS
- [ ] BINOCULARS
- [ ] HIKING GEAR
- [ ] BACKPACK

CAMPING *Checklist*

Entertainment

- [ ] BOARD GAMES
- [ ] CARDS
- [ ] RADIO
- [ ] SPORTS GEAR

Cleaning

- [ ] BROOM / MOP
- [ ] CLEANING SUPPLIES
- [ ] CLEANING CLOTHS
- [ ] DISH TOWELS

Misc

- [ ] COFFEE POT
- [ ] FIRE KETTLE
- [ ] COOLER & ICE
- [ ] FOLDABLE TABLE
- [ ] CAMPING CHAIRS
- [ ] LIGHTER / FUEL
- [ ] FIREWOOD
- [ ] BBQ GRLL
- [ ] GARBAGE BAGS

Shopping List

- [ ]
- [ ]
- [ ]
- [ ]
- [ ]
- [ ]
- [ ]
- [ ]
- [ ]
- [ ]
- [ ]
- [ ]
- [ ]
- [ ]
- [ ]
- [ ]
- [ ]
- [ ]
- [ ]
- [ ]

CAMPING MEAL *Planner*

MONDAY

TUESDAY

WEDNESDAY

THURSDAY

FRIDAY

SATURDAY

SUNDAY

SNACK IDEAS

CAMPING *Activities*

Monday

Tuesday

Wednesday

Thursday

Friday

Saturday

Sunday

MY CAMPING *Journal*

DATE:

WHAT I DID TODAY

HIGHLIGHT OF THE DAY

CAMPING *Memories*

DATE & CAMPSITE

WHAT WE DID

HIGHLIGHT OF THE TRIP

FISHING EXPEDITION
What I've Caught

LAKE / AREA	TYPE OF FISH	WEIGHT

FAMILY CAMPING
Adventures

CAMPGROUND

DATE

ACTIVITIES

HIGHLIGHT OF THE TRIP

FAVORITE MEMORY

HIKING CHECKLIST

CLOTHING

- [ ] HIKING BOOTS
- [ ] WOOL SOCKS
- [ ] BASE LAYERS
- [ ] SHORT SLEEVED SHIRT
- [ ] LONG SLEEVED SHIRT
- [ ] INSULATED MIDLAYER
- [ ] SUN HAT / VISOR
- [ ] BANDANA
- [ ] RAINWEAR
- [ ] WATCH

EQUIPMENT

- [ ] MAP
- [ ] COMPASS
- [ ] FLASHLIGHT
- [ ] HEAD LAMP
- [ ] LIGHTER / MATCHES
- [ ] KNIFE / MULTI-TOOL
- [ ] CELL PHONE
- [ ] POUCH
- [ ] MOLESKIN
- [ ] TREKKING POLES

FOOD & SUPPLIES

- [ ] MEALS & SNACKS
- [ ] WATER BOTTLE
- [ ] WATER TREATMENT
- [ ] COOKING POT
- [ ] COOKSTOVE/FUEL
- [ ] EATING UTENSILS
- [ ] BOWL/MUG/PLATE
- [ ] GARBAGE BAGS
- [ ] ROPE
- [ ] FOLDABLE BUCKET

CAMPING GEAR

- [ ] TENT
- [ ] SLEEPING BAG
- [ ] SLEEPING PAD
- [ ] TOILET PAPER
- [ ] BACKPACK
- [ ] DUCT TAPE
- [ ] FOLDING SAW
- [ ] POT LIFTER
- [ ] CAMP SHOES
- [ ] BEAR BANGER

MISC.

- [ ] INSECT REPELLENT
- [ ] LIP BALM
- [ ] FACE PROTECTOR
- [ ] EXTRA GLOVES
- [ ] DEODORANT
- [ ] HEADPHONES
- [ ] BATTERIES
- [ ] CHARGER
- [ ] DECK OF CARDS
- [ ] GPS

OTHER

- [ ] _____
- [ ] _____
- [ ] _____
- [ ] _____
- [ ] _____
- [ ] _____
- [ ] _____
- [ ] _____
- [ ] _____
- [ ] _____

HIKING JOURNAL

TRAIL		ELEVATION GAIN	LOSS
LOCATION			

DISTANCE	DURATION	START TIME	END TIME

TRAIL TYPE	DIFFICULTY	WEATHER	

IMPORTANT TRAIL DETAILS		NOTES	

TRAIL SURFACE	EXPOSURE		

CAMPING *Adventures*

COLOR IN THE DATES WHEN YOU WENT CAMPING

JANUARY

S	M	T	W	T	F	S

FEBRUARY

S	M	T	W	T	F	S

MARCH

S	M	T	W	T	F	S

APRIL

S	M	T	W	T	F	S

MAY

S	M	T	W	T	F	S

JUNE

S	M	T	W	T	F	S

JULY

S	M	T	W	T	F	S

AUGUST

S	M	T	W	T	F	S

SEPTEMBER

S	M	T	W	T	F	S

OCTOBER

S	M	T	W	T	F	S

NOVEMBER

S	M	T	W	T	F	S

DECEMBER

S	M	T	W	T	F	S

CAMPING TRACKER
Where I've Been

CAMPGROUND	LOCATION	DATE

CAMPING RESERVATION

CAMPGROUND PHONE #	RESERVATION DETAILS
CONTACT PERSON	
CAMPGROUND ADDRESS	ACTIVITIES
RESTAURANTS & AMENITIES	NOTES

SITE #	NIGHTLY RATE	CHECK IN	CHECK OUT

CAMPGROUND
Amenities

- WATER
- ELECTRIC
- SEWER
- WIFI
- CABLE TV
- PETS ALLOWED
- FIRE PIT
- SHOWERS
- TENTS PERMITTED
- VISITOR PARKING
- LAUNDRY SERVICES
- BBQ AREA
- SWIMMING
- ACCESS TO BEACH / LAKE
- BOAT LAUNCH
- FISHING

- POOL
- HOT TUB
- ACTIVITY CENTER
- NATURE TRAILS / HIKING
- PLAYGROUND
- BIKING / TRAILS
- GOLF COURSE
- KIDS CENTER
- FIREWORKS
- BINGO
- VOLLEYBALL
- TENNIS COURTS
- GARBAGE DISPOSAL
- CONVENIENCE STORE
- FIREWOOD/KINDLE
- PICNIC TABLES

CAMPING *Shopping List*

FAMILY CAMPING
Checklist

IMPORTANT GEAR

- ☐ Tent
- ☐ Backpack
- ☐ Tarp
- ☐ BBQ
- ☐ Sleeping Bag
- ☐ Camping Chairs
- ☐ _____
- ☐ _____
- ☐ _____
- ☐ _____
- ☐ _____

FOOD SUPPLIES

- ☐ Meals
- ☐ Snacks
- ☐ Water & Drinks
- ☐ Cook Set / Pots &
- ☐ Utensils & Dishes
- ☐ Condiments
- ☐ _____
- ☐ _____
- ☐ _____
- ☐ _____
- ☐ _____

CLOTHING

- ☐ Gloves & Hat
- ☐ Hats / Visors
- ☐ Socks & Underwear
- ☐ T-shirts & Sweaters
- ☐ Jacket / Raincoat
- ☐ Hiking Boots
- ☐ _____
- ☐ _____
- ☐ _____
- ☐ _____
- ☐ _____

TOOLS & SUPPLIES

- ☐ Lighter & Flashlights
- ☐ Firewood & Fire Starter
- ☐ Batteries
- ☐ Knife or Multi-Tool
- ☐ Compass
- ☐ _____
- ☐ _____
- ☐ _____
- ☐ _____
- ☐ _____

MISC ITEMS

- ☐ Garbage Bags
- ☐ Sunscreen
- ☐ Bug Spray/ Repellent
- ☐ Towels
- ☐ Water Bottle
- ☐ Toilet Paper
- ☐ _____
- ☐ _____
- ☐ _____
- ☐ _____
- ☐ _____

OTHER

- ☐ _____
- ☐ _____
- ☐ _____
- ☐ _____
- ☐ _____
- ☐ _____
- ☐ _____
- ☐ _____
- ☐ _____
- ☐ _____

FAMILY CAMPING

Checklist

IMPORTANT GEAR

- ☐ _____
- ☐ _____
- ☐ _____
- ☐ _____
- ☐ _____
- ☐ _____
- ☐ _____
- ☐ _____
- ☐ _____
- ☐ _____

FOOD SUPPLIES

- ☐ _____
- ☐ _____
- ☐ _____
- ☐ _____
- ☐ _____
- ☐ _____
- ☐ _____
- ☐ _____
- ☐ _____
- ☐ _____

CLOTHING

- ☐ _____
- ☐ _____
- ☐ _____
- ☐ _____
- ☐ _____
- ☐ _____
- ☐ _____
- ☐ _____
- ☐ _____
- ☐ _____

TOOLS & SUPPLIES

- ☐ _____
- ☐ _____
- ☐ _____
- ☐ _____
- ☐ _____
- ☐ _____
- ☐ _____
- ☐ _____
- ☐ _____
- ☐ _____

MISC ITEMS

- ☐ _____
- ☐ _____
- ☐ _____
- ☐ _____
- ☐ _____
- ☐ _____
- ☐ _____
- ☐ _____
- ☐ _____
- ☐ _____

OTHER

- ☐ _____
- ☐ _____
- ☐ _____
- ☐ _____
- ☐ _____
- ☐ _____
- ☐ _____
- ☐ _____
- ☐ _____
- ☐ _____

CAMPING SUPPLIES

CAMPING *Checklist*

Shelter

- [ ] TENT / CAMPER
- [ ] SLEEPING BLANKET
- [ ] PILLOWS
- [ ] TARP / COVERING

Comport

- [ ] SLEEPING BAGS
- [ ] SHEETS & PILLOWS
- [ ] AIR MATTRESS
- [ ] AIR PUMP

- [ ] HIKING BOOTS
- [ ] SWEATERS
- [ ] RAIN JACKET
- [ ] WARM SOCKS
- [ ] T-SHIRTS
- [ ] WARM COAT
- [ ] SUN VISOR / HAT
- [ ] BATHING SUIT
- [ ] PYJAMAS

Food

- [ ] FOOD / SUPPLIES
- [ ] CONDIMENTS
- [ ] COOKWARE/POTS
- [ ] TABLE CLOTH
- [ ] PLATES & CUPS
- [ ] UTENSILS
- [ ] PAPER TOWEL
- [ ] POT HOLDERS
- [ ] DISH SOAP
- [ ] CUTLERY

Personal

- [ ] SOAP
- [ ] SHAMPOO
- [ ] TOWELS
- [ ] TOOTHPASTE
- [ ] HAIR BRUSH
- [ ] SUNSCREEN
- [ ] DEODORANT
- [ ] HAND SANITIZER
- [ ] RAZORS

Essentials

- [ ] MEDICATION
- [ ] FIRST AID KIT
- [ ] TOILET PAPER
- [ ] LIP BALM
- [ ] TISSUES
- [ ] MIRROR
- [ ] HAIR CLIPS

Important

- [ ] BATTERIES
- [ ] CAMERA
- [ ] CHARGERS
- [ ] SUNGLASSES
- [ ] FLASHLIGHT
- [ ] BUG SPRAY
- [ ] LANTERNS
- [ ] COMPASS
- [ ] BINOCULARS
- [ ] HIKING GEAR
- [ ] BACKPACK

CAMPING *Checklist*

Entertainment

- [ ] BOARD GAMES
- [ ] CARDS
- [ ] RADIO
- [ ] SPORTS GEAR

Cleaning

- [ ] BROOM / MOP
- [ ] CLEANING SUPPLIES
- [ ] CLEANING CLOTHS
- [ ] DISH TOWELS

Misc

- [ ] COFFEE POT
- [ ] FIRE KETTLE
- [ ] COOLER & ICE
- [ ] FOLDABLE TABLE
- [ ] CAMPING CHAIRS
- [ ] LIGHTER / FUEL
- [ ] FIREWOOD
- [ ] BBQ GRLL
- [ ] GARBAGE BAGS

Shopping List

- [ ]
- [ ]
- [ ]
- [ ]
- [ ]
- [ ]
- [ ]
- [ ]
- [ ]
- [ ]
- [ ]
- [ ]
- [ ]
- [ ]
- [ ]
- [ ]
- [ ]
- [ ]
- [ ]
- [ ]
- [ ]
- [ ]

CAMPING MEAL *Planner*

MONDAY

TUESDAY

WEDNESDAY

THURSDAY

FRIDAY

SATURDAY

SUNDAY

SNACK IDEAS

CAMPING *Activities*

Monday

Tuesday

Wednesday

Thursday

Friday

Saturday

Sunday

MY CAMPING *Journal*

DATE:

WHAT I DID TODAY

HIGHLIGHT OF THE DAY

CAMPING *Memories*

DATE & CAMPSITE

WHAT WE DID

HIGHLIGHT OF THE TRIP

FISHING EXPEDITION
What I've Caught

LAKE / AREA	TYPE OF FISH	WEIGHT

FAMILY CAMPING
Adventures

CAMPGROUND

DATE

ACTIVITIES

HIGHLIGHT OF THE TRIP

FAVORITE MEMORY

HIKING CHECKLIST

CLOTHING

- [ ] HIKING BOOTS
- [ ] WOOL SOCKS
- [ ] BASE LAYERS
- [ ] SHORT SLEEVED SHIRT
- [ ] LONG SLEEVED SHIRT
- [ ] INSULATED MIDLAYER
- [ ] SUN HAT / VISOR
- [ ] BANDANA
- [ ] RAINWEAR
- [ ] WATCH

EQUIPMENT

- [ ] MAP
- [ ] COMPASS
- [ ] FLASHLIGHT
- [ ] HEAD LAMP
- [ ] LIGHTER / MATCHES
- [ ] KNIFE / MULTI-TOOL
- [ ] CELL PHONE
- [ ] POUCH
- [ ] MOLESKIN
- [ ] TREKKING POLES

FOOD & SUPPLIES

- [ ] MEALS & SNACKS
- [ ] WATER BOTTLE
- [ ] WATER TREATMENT
- [ ] COOKING POT
- [ ] COOKSTOVE/FUEL
- [ ] EATING UTENSILS
- [ ] BOWL/MUG/PLATE
- [ ] GARBAGE BAGS
- [ ] ROPE
- [ ] FOLDABLE BUCKET

CAMPING GEAR

- [ ] TENT
- [ ] SLEEPING BAG
- [ ] SLEEPING PAD
- [ ] TOILET PAPER
- [ ] BACKPACK
- [ ] DUCT TAPE
- [ ] FOLDING SAW
- [ ] POT LIFTER
- [ ] CAMP SHOES
- [ ] BEAR BANGER

MISC.

- [ ] INSECT REPELLENT
- [ ] LIP BALM
- [ ] FACE PROTECTOR
- [ ] EXTRA GLOVES
- [ ] DEODORANT
- [ ] HEADPHONES
- [ ] BATTERIES
- [ ] CHARGER
- [ ] DECK OF CARDS
- [ ] GPS

OTHER

- [ ] _____
- [ ] _____
- [ ] _____
- [ ] _____
- [ ] _____
- [ ] _____
- [ ] _____
- [ ] _____
- [ ] _____
- [ ] _____

HIKING JOURNAL

TRAIL		ELEVATION GAIN	LOSS
LOCATION			

DISTANCE	DURATION	START TIME	END TIME

TRAIL TYPE	DIFFICULTY	WEATHER	

IMPORTANT TRAIL DETAILS		NOTES	

TRAIL SURFACE	EXPOSURE		

CAMPING *Adventures*

COLOR IN THE DATES WHEN YOU WENT CAMPING

JANUARY

S	M	T	W	T	F	S

FEBRUARY

S	M	T	W	T	F	S

MARCH

S	M	T	W	T	F	S

APRIL

S	M	T	W	T	F	S

MAY

S	M	T	W	T	F	S

JUNE

S	M	T	W	T	F	S

JULY

S	M	T	W	T	F	S

AUGUST

S	M	T	W	T	F	S

SEPTEMBER

S	M	T	W	T	F	S

OCTOBER

S	M	T	W	T	F	S

NOVEMBER

S	M	T	W	T	F	S

DECEMBER

S	M	T	W	T	F	S

CAMPING TRACKER
Where I've Been

	CAMPGROUND	LOCATION	DATE
🔥			
🔥			
🔥			
🔥			
🔥			
🔥			
🔥			
🔥			
🔥			
🔥			
🔥			
🔥			
🔥			
🔥			
🔥			
🔥			
🔥			
🔥			
🔥			
🔥			

CAMPING RESERVATION

CAMPGROUND PHONE #	RESERVATION DETAILS
CONTACT PERSON	
CAMPGROUND ADDRESS	ACTIVITIES
RESTAURANTS & AMENITIES	NOTES

SITE #	NIGHTLY RATE	CHECK IN	CHECK OUT

CAMPGROUND
Amenities

- ○ WATER
- ○ ELECTRIC
- ○ SEWER
- ○ WIFI
- ○ CABLE TV
- ○ PETS ALLOWED
- ○ FIRE PIT
- ○ SHOWERS
- ○ TENTS PERMITTED
- ○ VISITOR PARKING
- ○ LAUNDRY SERVICES
- ○ BBQ AREA
- ○ SWIMMING
- ○ ACCESS TO BEACH / LAKE
- ○ BOAT LAUNCH
- ○ FISHING
- ○
- ○
- ○

- ○ POOL
- ○ HOT TUB
- ○ ACTIVITY CENTER
- ○ NATURE TRAILS / HIKING
- ○ PLAYGROUND
- ○ BIKING / TRAILS
- ○ GOLF COURSE
- ○ KIDS CENTER
- ○ FIREWORKS
- ○ BINGO
- ○ VOLLEYBALL
- ○ TENNIS COURTS
- ○ GARBAGE DISPOSAL
- ○ CONVENIENCE STORE
- ○ FIREWOOD/KINDLE
- ○ PICNIC TABLES
- ○
- ○
- ○

CAMPING *Shopping List*

FAMILY CAMPING
Checklist

IMPORTANT GEAR

- [ ] Tent
- [ ] Backpack
- [ ] Tarp
- [ ] BBQ
- [ ] Sleeping Bag
- [ ] Camping Chairs
- [ ] _____
- [ ] _____
- [ ] _____
- [ ] _____
- [ ] _____

FOOD SUPPLIES

- [ ] Meals
- [ ] Snacks
- [ ] Water & Drinks
- [ ] Cook Set / Pots &
- [ ] Utensils & Dishes
- [ ] Condiments
- [ ] _____
- [ ] _____
- [ ] _____
- [ ] _____
- [ ] _____

CLOTHING

- [ ] Gloves & Hat
- [ ] Hats / Visors
- [ ] Socks & Underwear
- [ ] T-shirts & Sweaters
- [ ] Jacket / Raincoat
- [ ] Hiking Boots
- [ ] _____
- [ ] _____
- [ ] _____
- [ ] _____
- [ ] _____

TOOLS & SUPPLIES

- [ ] Lighter & Flashlights
- [ ] Firewood & Fire Starter
- [ ] Batteries
- [ ] Knife or Multi-Tool
- [ ] Compass
- [ ] _____
- [ ] _____
- [ ] _____
- [ ] _____
- [ ] _____

MISC ITEMS

- [ ] Garbage Bags
- [ ] Sunscreen
- [ ] Bug Spray/ Repellent
- [ ] Towels
- [ ] Water Bottle
- [ ] Toilet Paper
- [ ] _____
- [ ] _____
- [ ] _____
- [ ] _____
- [ ] _____

OTHER

- [ ] _____
- [ ] _____
- [ ] _____
- [ ] _____
- [ ] _____
- [ ] _____
- [ ] _____
- [ ] _____
- [ ] _____
- [ ] _____

FAMILY CAMPING
Checklist

IMPORTANT GEAR

- [ ] _____
- [ ] _____
- [ ] _____
- [ ] _____
- [ ] _____
- [ ] _____
- [ ] _____
- [ ] _____
- [ ] _____
- [ ] _____

FOOD SUPPLIES

- [ ] _____
- [ ] _____
- [ ] _____
- [ ] _____
- [ ] _____
- [ ] _____
- [ ] _____
- [ ] _____
- [ ] _____
- [ ] _____

CLOTHING

- [ ] _____
- [ ] _____
- [ ] _____
- [ ] _____
- [ ] _____
- [ ] _____
- [ ] _____
- [ ] _____
- [ ] _____
- [ ] _____

TOOLS & SUPPLIES

- [ ] _____
- [ ] _____
- [ ] _____
- [ ] _____
- [ ] _____
- [ ] _____
- [ ] _____
- [ ] _____
- [ ] _____
- [ ] _____

MISC ITEMS

- [ ] _____
- [ ] _____
- [ ] _____
- [ ] _____
- [ ] _____
- [ ] _____
- [ ] _____
- [ ] _____
- [ ] _____
- [ ] _____

OTHER

- [ ] _____
- [ ] _____
- [ ] _____
- [ ] _____
- [ ] _____
- [ ] _____
- [ ] _____
- [ ] _____
- [ ] _____
- [ ] _____

CAMPING SUPPLIES

- [ ] _____
- [ ] _____
- [ ] _____
- [ ] _____
- [ ] _____
- [ ] _____
- [ ] _____
- [ ] _____
- [ ] _____
- [ ] _____
- [ ] _____
- [ ] _____
- [ ] _____
- [ ] _____
- [ ] _____
- [ ] _____
- [ ] _____
- [ ] _____
- [ ] _____
- [ ] _____
- [ ] _____
- [ ] _____

- [ ] _____
- [ ] _____
- [ ] _____
- [ ] _____
- [ ] _____
- [ ] _____
- [ ] _____
- [ ] _____
- [ ] _____
- [ ] _____
- [ ] _____
- [ ] _____
- [ ] _____
- [ ] _____
- [ ] _____
- [ ] _____
- [ ] _____
- [ ] _____
- [ ] _____
- [ ] _____
- [ ] _____
- [ ] _____

- [ ] _____
- [ ] _____
- [ ] _____
- [ ] _____
- [ ] _____
- [ ] _____
- [ ] _____
- [ ] _____
- [ ] _____
- [ ] _____
- [ ] _____
- [ ] _____
- [ ] _____
- [ ] _____
- [ ] _____
- [ ] _____
- [ ] _____
- [ ] _____
- [ ] _____
- [ ] _____
- [ ] _____
- [ ] _____

CAMPING *Checklist*

Shelter

- [ ] TENT / CAMPER
- [ ] SLEEPING BLANKET
- [ ] PILLOWS
- [ ] TARP / COVERING

Comport

- [ ] SLEEPING BAGS
- [ ] SHEETS & PILLOWS
- [ ] AIR MATTRESS
- [ ] AIR PUMP

- [ ] HIKING BOOTS
- [ ] SWEATERS
- [ ] RAIN JACKET
- [ ] WARM SOCKS
- [ ] T-SHIRTS
- [ ] WARM COAT
- [ ] SUN VISOR / HAT
- [ ] BATHING SUIT
- [ ] PYJAMAS

Food

- [ ] FOOD / SUPPLIES
- [ ] CONDIMENTS
- [ ] COOKWARE/POTS
- [ ] TABLE CLOTH
- [ ] PLATES & CUPS
- [ ] UTENSILS
- [ ] PAPER TOWEL
- [ ] POT HOLDERS
- [ ] DISH SOAP
- [ ] CUTLERY

Personal

- [ ] SOAP
- [ ] SHAMPOO
- [ ] TOWELS
- [ ] TOOTHPASTE
- [ ] HAIR BRUSH
- [ ] SUNSCREEN
- [ ] DEODORANT
- [ ] HAND SANITIZER
- [ ] RAZORS

Essentials

- [ ] MEDICATION
- [ ] FIRST AID KIT
- [ ] TOILET PAPER
- [ ] LIP BALM
- [ ] TISSUES
- [ ] MIRROR
- [ ] HAIR CLIPS

Important

- [ ] BATTERIES
- [ ] CAMERA
- [ ] CHARGERS
- [ ] SUNGLASSES
- [ ] FLASHLIGHT
- [ ] BUG SPRAY
- [ ] LANTERNS
- [ ] COMPASS
- [ ] BINOCULARS
- [ ] HIKING GEAR
- [ ] BACKPACK

CAMPING *Checklist*

Entertainment

- [ ] BOARD GAMES
- [ ] CARDS
- [ ] RADIO
- [ ] SPORTS GEAR

Cleaning

- [ ] BROOM / MOP
- [ ] CLEANING SUPPLIES
- [ ] CLEANING CLOTHS
- [ ] DISH TOWELS

Misc

- [ ] COFFEE POT
- [ ] FIRE KETTLE
- [ ] COOLER & ICE
- [ ] FOLDABLE TABLE
- [ ] CAMPING CHAIRS
- [ ] LIGHTER / FUEL
- [ ] FIREWOOD
- [ ] BBQ GRLL
- [ ] GARBAGE BAGS

Shopping List

- [ ]
- [ ]
- [ ]
- [ ]
- [ ]
- [ ]
- [ ]
- [ ]
- [ ]
- [ ]
- [ ]
- [ ]
- [ ]
- [ ]
- [ ]
- [ ]
- [ ]
- [ ]
- [ ]

CAMPING MEAL *Planner*

MONDAY

TUESDAY

WEDNESDAY

THURSDAY

FRIDAY

SATURDAY

SUNDAY

SNACK IDEAS

CAMPING *Activities*

Monday

Tuesday

Wednesday

Thursday

Friday

Saturday

Sunday

MY CAMPING *Journal*

DATE:

WHAT I DID TODAY

HIGHLIGHT OF THE DAY

CAMPING *Memories*

DATE & CAMPSITE

WHAT WE DID

HIGHLIGHT OF THE TRIP

FISHING EXPEDITION
What I've Caught

LAKE / AREA	TYPE OF FISH	WEIGHT

FAMILY CAMPING
Adventures

CAMPGROUND

DATE

ACTIVITIES

HIGHLIGHT OF THE TRIP

FAVORITE MEMORY

HIKING CHECKLIST

CLOTHING

- ☐ HIKING BOOTS
- ☐ WOOL SOCKS
- ☐ BASE LAYERS
- ☐ SHORT SLEEVED SHIRT
- ☐ LONG SLEEVED SHIRT
- ☐ INSULATED MIDLAYER
- ☐ SUN HAT / VISOR
- ☐ BANDANA
- ☐ RAINWEAR
- ☐ WATCH

EQUIPMENT

- ☐ MAP
- ☐ COMPASS
- ☐ FLASHLIGHT
- ☐ HEAD LAMP
- ☐ LIGHTER / MATCHES
- ☐ KNIFE / MULTI-TOOL
- ☐ CELL PHONE
- ☐ POUCH
- ☐ MOLESKIN
- ☐ TREKKING POLES

FOOD & SUPPLIES

- ☐ MEALS & SNACKS
- ☐ WATER BOTTLE
- ☐ WATER TREATMENT
- ☐ COOKING POT
- ☐ COOKSTOVE/FUEL
- ☐ EATING UTENSILS
- ☐ BOWL/MUG/PLATE
- ☐ GARBAGE BAGS
- ☐ ROPE
- ☐ FOLDABLE BUCKET

CAMPING GEAR

- ☐ TENT
- ☐ SLEEPING BAG
- ☐ SLEEPING PAD
- ☐ TOILET PAPER
- ☐ BACKPACK
- ☐ DUCT TAPE
- ☐ FOLDING SAW
- ☐ POT LIFTER
- ☐ CAMP SHOES
- ☐ BEAR BANGER

MISC.

- ☐ INSECT REPELLENT
- ☐ LIP BALM
- ☐ FACE PROTECTOR
- ☐ EXTRA GLOVES
- ☐ DEODORANT
- ☐ HEADPHONES
- ☐ BATTERIES
- ☐ CHARGER
- ☐ DECK OF CARDS
- ☐ GPS

OTHER

- ☐ _____
- ☐ _____
- ☐ _____
- ☐ _____
- ☐ _____
- ☐ _____
- ☐ _____
- ☐ _____
- ☐ _____
- ☐ _____

HIKING JOURNAL

TRAIL	ELEVATION GAIN	LOSS
LOCATION		

DISTANCE	DURATION	START TIME	END TIME

TRAIL TYPE	DIFFICULTY	WEATHER	

IMPORTANT TRAIL DETAILS		NOTES	

TRAIL SURFACE	EXPOSURE		

CAMPING *Adventures*

COLOR IN THE DATES WHEN YOU WENT CAMPING

JANUARY
S	M	T	W	T	F	S

FEBRUARY
S	M	T	W	T	F	S

MARCH
S	M	T	W	T	F	S

APRIL
S	M	T	W	T	F	S

MAY
S	M	T	W	T	F	S

JUNE
S	M	T	W	T	F	S

JULY
S	M	T	W	T	F	S

AUGUST
S	M	T	W	T	F	S

SEPTEMBER
S	M	T	W	T	F	S

OCTOBER
S	M	T	W	T	F	S

NOVEMBER
S	M	T	W	T	F	S

DECEMBER
S	M	T	W	T	F	S

CAMPING TRACKER
Where I've Been

CAMPGROUND	LOCATION	DATE

CAMPING RESERVATION

CAMPGROUND PHONE #	RESERVATION DETAILS
CONTACT PERSON	
CAMPGROUND ADDRESS	ACTIVITIES
RESTAURANTS & AMENITIES	NOTES

SITE #	NIGHTLY RATE	CHECK IN	CHECK OUT

CAMPGROUND
Amenities

- WATER
- ELECTRIC
- SEWER
- WIFI
- CABLE TV
- PETS ALLOWED
- FIRE PIT
- SHOWERS
- TENTS PERMITTED
- VISITOR PARKING
- LAUNDRY SERVICES
- BBQ AREA
- SWIMMING
- ACCESS TO BEACH / LAKE
- BOAT LAUNCH
- FISHING

- POOL
- HOT TUB
- ACTIVITY CENTER
- NATURE TRAILS / HIKING
- PLAYGROUND
- BIKING / TRAILS
- GOLF COURSE
- KIDS CENTER
- FIREWORKS
- BINGO
- VOLLEYBALL
- TENNIS COURTS
- GARBAGE DISPOSAL
- CONVENIENCE STORE
- FIREWOOD/KINDLE
- PICNIC TABLES

CAMPING *Shopping List*

FAMILY CAMPING
Checklist

IMPORTANT GEAR

- [ ] Tent
- [ ] Backpack
- [ ] Tarp
- [ ] BBQ
- [ ] Sleeping Bag
- [ ] Camping Chairs
- [ ] _____
- [ ] _____
- [ ] _____
- [ ] _____
- [ ] _____

FOOD SUPPLIES

- [ ] Meals
- [ ] Snacks
- [ ] Water & Drinks
- [ ] Cook Set / Pots &
- [ ] Utensils & Dishes
- [ ] Condiments
- [ ] _____
- [ ] _____
- [ ] _____
- [ ] _____
- [ ] _____

CLOTHING

- [ ] Gloves & Hat
- [ ] Hats / Visors
- [ ] Socks & Underwear
- [ ] T-shirts & Sweaters
- [ ] Jacket / Raincoat
- [ ] Hiking Boots
- [ ] _____
- [ ] _____
- [ ] _____
- [ ] _____
- [ ] _____

TOOLS & SUPPLIES

- [ ] Lighter & Flashlights
- [ ] Firewood & Fire Starter
- [ ] Batteries
- [ ] Knife or Multi-Tool
- [ ] Compass
- [ ] _____
- [ ] _____
- [ ] _____
- [ ] _____
- [ ] _____

MISC ITEMS

- [ ] Garbage Bags
- [ ] Sunscreen
- [ ] Bug Spray/ Repellent
- [ ] Towels
- [ ] Water Bottle
- [ ] Toilet Paper
- [ ] _____
- [ ] _____
- [ ] _____
- [ ] _____

OTHER

- [ ] _____
- [ ] _____
- [ ] _____
- [ ] _____
- [ ] _____
- [ ] _____
- [ ] _____
- [ ] _____
- [ ] _____

FAMILY CAMPING

Checklist

IMPORTANT GEAR

- [ ] _____
- [ ] _____
- [ ] _____
- [ ] _____
- [ ] _____
- [ ] _____
- [ ] _____
- [ ] _____
- [ ] _____
- [ ] _____

FOOD SUPPLIES

- [ ] _____
- [ ] _____
- [ ] _____
- [ ] _____
- [ ] _____
- [ ] _____
- [ ] _____
- [ ] _____
- [ ] _____
- [ ] _____

CLOTHING

- [ ] _____
- [ ] _____
- [ ] _____
- [ ] _____
- [ ] _____
- [ ] _____
- [ ] _____
- [ ] _____
- [ ] _____

TOOLS & SUPPLIES

- [ ] _____
- [ ] _____
- [ ] _____
- [ ] _____
- [ ] _____
- [ ] _____
- [ ] _____
- [ ] _____
- [ ] _____
- [ ] _____

MISC ITEMS

- [ ] _____
- [ ] _____
- [ ] _____
- [ ] _____
- [ ] _____
- [ ] _____
- [ ] _____
- [ ] _____
- [ ] _____
- [ ] _____

OTHER

- [ ] _____
- [ ] _____
- [ ] _____
- [ ] _____
- [ ] _____
- [ ] _____
- [ ] _____
- [ ] _____
- [ ] _____
- [ ] _____

CAMPING SUPPLIES

- [ ] _____
- [ ] _____
- [ ] _____
- [ ] _____
- [ ] _____
- [ ] _____
- [ ] _____
- [ ] _____
- [ ] _____
- [ ] _____
- [ ] _____
- [ ] _____
- [ ] _____
- [ ] _____
- [ ] _____
- [ ] _____
- [ ] _____
- [ ] _____
- [ ] _____
- [ ] _____
- [ ] _____

- [ ] _____
- [ ] _____
- [ ] _____
- [ ] _____
- [ ] _____
- [ ] _____
- [ ] _____
- [ ] _____
- [ ] _____
- [ ] _____
- [ ] _____
- [ ] _____
- [ ] _____
- [ ] _____
- [ ] _____
- [ ] _____
- [ ] _____
- [ ] _____
- [ ] _____
- [ ] _____
- [ ] _____

- [ ] _____
- [ ] _____
- [ ] _____
- [ ] _____
- [ ] _____
- [ ] _____
- [ ] _____
- [ ] _____
- [ ] _____
- [ ] _____
- [ ] _____
- [ ] _____
- [ ] _____
- [ ] _____
- [ ] _____
- [ ] _____
- [ ] _____
- [ ] _____
- [ ] _____
- [ ] _____
- [ ] _____

CAMPING *Checklist*

Shelter

- [ ] TENT / CAMPER
- [ ] SLEEPING BLANKET
- [ ] PILLOWS
- [ ] TARP / COVERING

Comport

- [ ] SLEEPING BAGS
- [ ] SHEETS & PILLOWS
- [ ] AIR MATTRESS
- [ ] AIR PUMP

- [ ] HIKING BOOTS
- [ ] SWEATERS
- [ ] RAIN JACKET
- [ ] WARM SOCKS
- [ ] T-SHIRTS
- [ ] WARM COAT
- [ ] SUN VISOR / HAT
- [ ] BATHING SUIT
- [ ] PYJAMAS

Food

- [ ] FOOD / SUPPLIES
- [ ] CONDIMENTS
- [ ] COOKWARE/POTS
- [ ] TABLE CLOTH
- [ ] PLATES & CUPS
- [ ] UTENSILS
- [ ] PAPER TOWEL
- [ ] POT HOLDERS
- [ ] DISH SOAP
- [ ] CUTLERY

Personal

- [ ] SOAP
- [ ] SHAMPOO
- [ ] TOWELS
- [ ] TOOTHPASTE
- [ ] HAIR BRUSH
- [ ] SUNSCREEN
- [ ] DEODORANT
- [ ] HAND SANITIZER
- [ ] RAZORS

Essentials

- [ ] MEDICATION
- [ ] FIRST AID KIT
- [ ] TOILET PAPER
- [ ] LIP BALM
- [ ] TISSUES
- [ ] MIRROR
- [ ] HAIR CLIPS

Important

- [ ] BATTERIES
- [ ] CAMERA
- [ ] CHARGERS
- [ ] SUNGLASSES
- [ ] FLASHLIGHT
- [ ] BUG SPRAY
- [ ] LANTERNS
- [ ] COMPASS
- [ ] BINOCULARS
- [ ] HIKING GEAR
- [ ] BACKPACK

CAMPING *Checklist*

Entertainment

- [ ] BOARD GAMES
- [ ] CARDS
- [ ] RADIO
- [ ] SPORTS GEAR

Cleaning

- [ ] BROOM / MOP
- [ ] CLEANING SUPPLIES
- [ ] CLEANING CLOTHS
- [ ] DISH TOWELS

Misc

- [ ] COFFEE POT
- [ ] FIRE KETTLE
- [ ] COOLER & ICE
- [ ] FOLDABLE TABLE
- [ ] CAMPING CHAIRS
- [ ] LIGHTER / FUEL
- [ ] FIREWOOD
- [ ] BBQ GRLL
- [ ] GARBAGE BAGS

Shopping List

- [ ]
- [ ]
- [ ]
- [ ]
- [ ]
- [ ]
- [ ]
- [ ]
- [ ]
- [ ]
- [ ]
- [ ]
- [ ]
- [ ]
- [ ]
- [ ]
- [ ]
- [ ]
- [ ]
- [ ]
- [ ]

CAMPING MEAL *Planner*

MONDAY

TUESDAY

WEDNESDAY

THURSDAY

FRIDAY

SATURDAY

SUNDAY

SNACK IDEAS

CAMPING *Activities*

Monday

Tuesday

Wednesday

Thursday

Friday

Saturday

Sunday

MY CAMPING *Journal*

DATE:

WHAT I DID TODAY

HIGHLIGHT OF THE DAY

CAMPING *Memories*

DATE & CAMPSITE

WHAT WE DID

HIGHLIGHT OF THE TRIP

FISHING EXPEDITION
What I've Caught

LAKE / AREA	TYPE OF FISH	WEIGHT

FAMILY CAMPING
Adventures

CAMPGROUND

DATE

ACTIVITIES

HIGHLIGHT OF THE TRIP

FAVORITE MEMORY

HIKING CHECKLIST

CLOTHING

- ☐ HIKING BOOTS
- ☐ WOOL SOCKS
- ☐ BASE LAYERS
- ☐ SHORT SLEEVED SHIRT
- ☐ LONG SLEEVED SHIRT
- ☐ INSULATED MIDLAYER
- ☐ SUN HAT / VISOR
- ☐ BANDANA
- ☐ RAINWEAR
- ☐ WATCH

EQUIPMENT

- ☐ MAP
- ☐ COMPASS
- ☐ FLASHLIGHT
- ☐ HEAD LAMP
- ☐ LIGHTER / MATCHES
- ☐ KNIFE / MULTI-TOOL
- ☐ CELL PHONE
- ☐ POUCH
- ☐ MOLESKIN
- ☐ TREKKING POLES

FOOD & SUPPLIES

- ☐ MEALS & SNACKS
- ☐ WATER BOTTLE
- ☐ WATER TREATMENT
- ☐ COOKING POT
- ☐ COOKSTOVE/FUEL
- ☐ EATING UTENSILS
- ☐ BOWL/MUG/PLATE
- ☐ GARBAGE BAGS
- ☐ ROPE
- ☐ FOLDABLE BUCKET

CAMPING GEAR

- ☐ TENT
- ☐ SLEEPING BAG
- ☐ SLEEPING PAD
- ☐ TOILET PAPER
- ☐ BACKPACK
- ☐ DUCT TAPE
- ☐ FOLDING SAW
- ☐ POT LIFTER
- ☐ CAMP SHOES
- ☐ BEAR BANGER

MISC.

- ☐ INSECT REPELLENT
- ☐ LIP BALM
- ☐ FACE PROTECTOR
- ☐ EXTRA GLOVES
- ☐ DEODORANT
- ☐ HEADPHONES
- ☐ BATTERIES
- ☐ CHARGER
- ☐ DECK OF CARDS
- ☐ GPS

OTHER

- ☐ _____
- ☐ _____
- ☐ _____
- ☐ _____
- ☐ _____
- ☐ _____
- ☐ _____
- ☐ _____
- ☐ _____
- ☐ _____

HIKING JOURNAL

TRAIL		ELEVATION GAIN	LOSS
LOCATION			

DISTANCE	DURATION	START TIME	END TIME

TRAIL TYPE	DIFFICULTY	WEATHER	

IMPORTANT TRAIL DETAILS	NOTES

TRAIL SURFACE	EXPOSURE	

CAMPING *Adventures*

COLOR IN THE DATES WHEN YOU WENT CAMPING

JANUARY

S	M	T	W	T	F	S

FEBRUARY

S	M	T	W	T	F	S

MARCH

S	M	T	W	T	F	S

APRIL

S	M	T	W	T	F	S

MAY

S	M	T	W	T	F	S

JUNE

S	M	T	W	T	F	S

JULY

S	M	T	W	T	F	S

AUGUST

S	M	T	W	T	F	S

SEPTEMBER

S	M	T	W	T	F	S

OCTOBER

S	M	T	W	T	F	S

NOVEMBER

S	M	T	W	T	F	S

DECEMBER

S	M	T	W	T	F	S

CAMPING TRACKER
Where I've Been

	CAMPGROUND	LOCATION	DATE

CAMPING RESERVATION

CAMPGROUND PHONE #	RESERVATION DETAILS
CONTACT PERSON	

CAMPGROUND ADDRESS	ACTIVITIES

RESTAURANTS & AMENITIES	NOTES

SITE #	NIGHTLY RATE	CHECK IN	CHECK OUT

CAMPGROUND
Amenities

- WATER
- ELECTRIC
- SEWER
- WIFI
- CABLE TV
- PETS ALLOWED
- FIRE PIT
- SHOWERS
- TENTS PERMITTED
- VISITOR PARKING
- LAUNDRY SERVICES
- BBQ AREA
- SWIMMING
- ACCESS TO BEACH / LAKE
- BOAT LAUNCH
- FISHING

- POOL
- HOT TUB
- ACTIVITY CENTER
- NATURE TRAILS / HIKING
- PLAYGROUND
- BIKING / TRAILS
- GOLF COURSE
- KIDS CENTER
- FIREWORKS
- BINGO
- VOLLEYBALL
- TENNIS COURTS
- GARBAGE DISPOSAL
- CONVENIENCE STORE
- FIREWOOD/KINDLE
- PICNIC TABLES

CAMPING *Shopping List*

FAMILY CAMPING
Checklist

IMPORTANT GEAR

- [ ] Tent
- [ ] Backpack
- [ ] Tarp
- [ ] BBQ
- [ ] Sleeping Bag
- [ ] Camping Chairs
- [ ] _____
- [ ] _____
- [ ] _____
- [ ] _____
- [ ] _____

FOOD SUPPLIES

- [ ] Meals
- [ ] Snacks
- [ ] Water & Drinks
- [ ] Cook Set / Pots &
- [ ] Utensils & Dishes
- [ ] Condiments
- [ ] _____
- [ ] _____
- [ ] _____
- [ ] _____
- [ ] _____

CLOTHING

- [ ] Gloves & Hat
- [ ] Hats / Visors
- [ ] Socks & Underwear
- [ ] T-shirts & Sweaters
- [ ] Jacket / Raincoat
- [ ] Hiking Boots
- [ ] _____
- [ ] _____
- [ ] _____
- [ ] _____
- [ ] _____

TOOLS & SUPPLIES

- [ ] Lighter & Flashlights
- [ ] Firewood & Fire Starter
- [ ] Batteries
- [ ] Knife or Multi-Tool
- [ ] Compass
- [ ] _____
- [ ] _____
- [ ] _____
- [ ] _____
- [ ] _____

MISC ITEMS

- [ ] Garbage Bags
- [ ] Sunscreen
- [ ] Bug Spray/ Repellent
- [ ] Towels
- [ ] Water Bottle
- [ ] Toilet Paper
- [ ] _____
- [ ] _____
- [ ] _____
- [ ] _____

OTHER

- [ ] _____
- [ ] _____
- [ ] _____
- [ ] _____
- [ ] _____
- [ ] _____
- [ ] _____
- [ ] _____
- [ ] _____

FAMILY CAMPING

Checklist

IMPORTANT GEAR

- [ ] _____
- [ ] _____
- [ ] _____
- [ ] _____
- [ ] _____
- [ ] _____
- [ ] _____
- [ ] _____
- [ ] _____
- [ ] _____

FOOD SUPPLIES

- [ ] _____
- [ ] _____
- [ ] _____
- [ ] _____
- [ ] _____
- [ ] _____
- [ ] _____
- [ ] _____
- [ ] _____
- [ ] _____

CLOTHING

- [ ] _____
- [ ] _____
- [ ] _____
- [ ] _____
- [ ] _____
- [ ] _____
- [ ] _____
- [ ] _____
- [ ] _____
- [ ] _____

TOOLS & SUPPLIES

- [ ] _____
- [ ] _____
- [ ] _____
- [ ] _____
- [ ] _____
- [ ] _____
- [ ] _____
- [ ] _____
- [ ] _____
- [ ] _____

MISC ITEMS

- [ ] _____
- [ ] _____
- [ ] _____
- [ ] _____
- [ ] _____
- [ ] _____
- [ ] _____
- [ ] _____
- [ ] _____
- [ ] _____

OTHER

- [ ] _____
- [ ] _____
- [ ] _____
- [ ] _____
- [ ] _____
- [ ] _____
- [ ] _____
- [ ] _____
- [ ] _____
- [ ] _____

CAMPING SUPPLIES

- [ ] _____
- [ ] _____
- [ ] _____
- [ ] _____
- [ ] _____
- [ ] _____
- [ ] _____
- [ ] _____
- [ ] _____
- [ ] _____
- [ ] _____
- [ ] _____
- [ ] _____
- [ ] _____
- [ ] _____
- [ ] _____
- [ ] _____
- [ ] _____
- [ ] _____
- [ ] _____
- [ ] _____
- [ ] _____
- [ ] _____

- [ ] _____
- [ ] _____
- [ ] _____
- [ ] _____
- [ ] _____
- [ ] _____
- [ ] _____
- [ ] _____
- [ ] _____
- [ ] _____
- [ ] _____
- [ ] _____
- [ ] _____
- [ ] _____
- [ ] _____
- [ ] _____
- [ ] _____
- [ ] _____
- [ ] _____
- [ ] _____
- [ ] _____
- [ ] _____
- [ ] _____

- [ ] _____
- [ ] _____
- [ ] _____
- [ ] _____
- [ ] _____
- [ ] _____
- [ ] _____
- [ ] _____
- [ ] _____
- [ ] _____
- [ ] _____
- [ ] _____
- [ ] _____
- [ ] _____
- [ ] _____
- [ ] _____
- [ ] _____
- [ ] _____
- [ ] _____
- [ ] _____
- [ ] _____
- [ ] _____
- [ ] _____

CAMPING *Checklist*

Shelter
- TENT / CAMPER
- SLEEPING BLANKET
- PILLOWS
- TARP / COVERING

Comport
- SLEEPING BAGS
- SHEETS & PILLOWS
- AIR MATTRESS
- AIR PUMP

- HIKING BOOTS
- SWEATERS
- RAIN JACKET
- WARM SOCKS
- T-SHIRTS
- WARM COAT
- SUN VISOR / HAT
- BATHING SUIT
- PYJAMAS

Food
- FOOD / SUPPLIES
- CONDIMENTS
- COOKWARE/POTS
- TABLE CLOTH
- PLATES & CUPS
- UTENSILS
- PAPER TOWEL
- POT HOLDERS
- DISH SOAP
- CUTLERY

Personal
- SOAP
- SHAMPOO
- TOWELS
- TOOTHPASTE
- HAIR BRUSH
- SUNSCREEN
- DEODORANT
- HAND SANITIZER
- RAZORS

Essentials
- MEDICATION
- FIRST AID KIT
- TOILET PAPER
- LIP BALM
- TISSUES
- MIRROR
- HAIR CLIPS

Important
- BATTERIES
- CAMERA
- CHARGERS
- SUNGLASSES
- FLASHLIGHT
- BUG SPRAY
- LANTERNS
- COMPASS
- BINOCULARS
- HIKING GEAR
- BACKPACK

CAMPING *Checklist*

Entertainment

- [ ] BOARD GAMES
- [ ] CARDS
- [ ] RADIO
- [ ] SPORTS GEAR

Cleaning

- [ ] BROOM / MOP
- [ ] CLEANING SUPPLIES
- [ ] CLEANING CLOTHS
- [ ] DISH TOWELS

Misc

- [ ] COFFEE POT
- [ ] FIRE KETTLE
- [ ] COOLER & ICE
- [ ] FOLDABLE TABLE
- [ ] CAMPING CHAIRS
- [ ] LIGHTER / FUEL
- [ ] FIREWOOD
- [ ] BBQ GRLL
- [ ] GARBAGE BAGS

Shopping List

- [ ]
- [ ]
- [ ]
- [ ]
- [ ]
- [ ]
- [ ]
- [ ]
- [ ]
- [ ]
- [ ]
- [ ]
- [ ]
- [ ]
- [ ]
- [ ]
- [ ]
- [ ]
- [ ]
- [ ]
- [ ]
- [ ]

CAMPING MEAL *Planner*

MONDAY

TUESDAY

WEDNESDAY

THURSDAY

FRIDAY

SATURDAY

SUNDAY

SNACK IDEAS

CAMPING *Activities*

Monday

Tuesday

Wednesday

Thursday

Friday

Saturday

Sunday

MY CAMPING *Journal*

DATE:

WHAT I DID TODAY

HIGHLIGHT OF THE DAY

CAMPING *Memories*

DATE & CAMPSITE

WHAT WE DID

HIGHLIGHT OF THE TRIP

FISHING EXPEDITION
What I've Caught

LAKE / AREA	TYPE OF FISH	WEIGHT

FAMILY CAMPING
Adventures

CAMPGROUND

DATE

ACTIVITIES

HIGHLIGHT OF THE TRIP

FAVORITE MEMORY

HIKING CHECKLIST

CLOTHING

- [ ] HIKING BOOTS
- [ ] WOOL SOCKS
- [ ] BASE LAYERS
- [ ] SHORT SLEEVED SHIRT
- [ ] LONG SLEEVED SHIRT
- [ ] INSULATED MIDLAYER
- [ ] SUN HAT / VISOR
- [ ] BANDANA
- [ ] RAINWEAR
- [ ] WATCH

EQUIPMENT

- [ ] MAP
- [ ] COMPASS
- [ ] FLASHLIGHT
- [ ] HEAD LAMP
- [ ] LIGHTER / MATCHES
- [ ] KNIFE / MULTI-TOOL
- [ ] CELL PHONE
- [ ] POUCH
- [ ] MOLESKIN
- [ ] TREKKING POLES

FOOD & SUPPLIES

- [ ] MEALS & SNACKS
- [ ] WATER BOTTLE
- [ ] WATER TREATMENT
- [ ] COOKING POT
- [ ] COOKSTOVE/FUEL
- [ ] EATING UTENSILS
- [ ] BOWL/MUG/PLATE
- [ ] GARBAGE BAGS
- [ ] ROPE
- [ ] FOLDABLE BUCKET

CAMPING GEAR

- [ ] TENT
- [ ] SLEEPING BAG
- [ ] SLEEPING PAD
- [ ] TOILET PAPER
- [ ] BACKPACK
- [ ] DUCT TAPE
- [ ] FOLDING SAW
- [ ] POT LIFTER
- [ ] CAMP SHOES
- [ ] BEAR BANGER

MISC.

- [ ] INSECT REPELLENT
- [ ] LIP BALM
- [ ] FACE PROTECTOR
- [ ] EXTRA GLOVES
- [ ] DEODORANT
- [ ] HEADPHONES
- [ ] BATTERIES
- [ ] CHARGER
- [ ] DECK OF CARDS
- [ ] GPS

OTHER

- [ ] _____
- [ ] _____
- [ ] _____
- [ ] _____
- [ ] _____
- [ ] _____
- [ ] _____
- [ ] _____
- [ ] _____
- [ ] _____

HIKING JOURNAL

TRAIL		ELEVATION GAIN	LOSS
LOCATION			

DISTANCE	DURATION	START TIME	END TIME

TRAIL TYPE	DIFFICULTY	WEATHER	

IMPORTANT TRAIL DETAILS	NOTES

TRAIL SURFACE	EXPOSURE	

CAMPING *Adventures*

COLOR IN THE DATES WHEN YOU WENT CAMPING

JANUARY

S	M	T	W	T	F	S

FEBRUARY

S	M	T	W	T	F	S

MARCH

S	M	T	W	T	F	S

APRIL

S	M	T	W	T	F	S

MAY

S	M	T	W	T	F	S

JUNE

S	M	T	W	T	F	S

JULY

S	M	T	W	T	F	S

AUGUST

S	M	T	W	T	F	S

SEPTEMBER

S	M	T	W	T	F	S

OCTOBER

S	M	T	W	T	F	S

NOVEMBER

S	M	T	W	T	F	S

DECEMBER

S	M	T	W	T	F	S

CAMPING TRACKER
Where I've Been

CAMPGROUND	LOCATION	DATE

CAMPING RESERVATION

CAMPGROUND PHONE #	RESERVATION DETAILS
CONTACT PERSON	
CAMPGROUND ADDRESS	ACTIVITIES
RESTAURANTS & AMENITIES	NOTES

SITE #	NIGHTLY RATE	CHECK IN	CHECK OUT

CAMPGROUND
Amenities

- WATER
- ELECTRIC
- SEWER
- WIFI
- CABLE TV
- PETS ALLOWED
- FIRE PIT
- SHOWERS
- TENTS PERMITTED
- VISITOR PARKING
- LAUNDRY SERVICES
- BBQ AREA
- SWIMMING
- ACCESS TO BEACH / LAKE
- BOAT LAUNCH
- FISHING

- POOL
- HOT TUB
- ACTIVITY CENTER
- NATURE TRAILS / HIKING
- PLAYGROUND
- BIKING / TRAILS
- GOLF COURSE
- KIDS CENTER
- FIREWORKS
- BINGO
- VOLLEYBALL
- TENNIS COURTS
- GARBAGE DISPOSAL
- CONVENIENCE STORE
- FIREWOOD/KINDLE
- PICNIC TABLES

CAMPING *Shopping List*

FAMILY CAMPING
Checklist

IMPORTANT GEAR

- ☐ Tent
- ☐ Backpack
- ☐ Tarp
- ☐ BBQ
- ☐ Sleeping Bag
- ☐ Camping Chairs
- ☐ _____
- ☐ _____
- ☐ _____
- ☐ _____
- ☐ _____

FOOD SUPPLIES

- ☐ Meals
- ☐ Snacks
- ☐ Water & Drinks
- ☐ Cook Set / Pots &
- ☐ Utensils & Dishes
- ☐ Condiments
- ☐ _____
- ☐ _____
- ☐ _____
- ☐ _____
- ☐ _____

CLOTHING

- ☐ Gloves & Hat
- ☐ Hats / Visors
- ☐ Socks & Underwear
- ☐ T-shirts & Sweaters
- ☐ Jacket / Raincoat
- ☐ Hiking Boots
- ☐ _____
- ☐ _____
- ☐ _____
- ☐ _____
- ☐ _____

TOOLS & SUPPLIES

- ☐ Lighter & Flashlights
- ☐ Firewood & Fire Starter
- ☐ Batteries
- ☐ Knife or Multi-Tool
- ☐ Compass
- ☐ _____
- ☐ _____
- ☐ _____
- ☐ _____
- ☐ _____

MISC ITEMS

- ☐ Garbage Bags
- ☐ Sunscreen
- ☐ Bug Spray/ Repellent
- ☐ Towels
- ☐ Water Bottle
- ☐ Toilet Paper
- ☐ _____
- ☐ _____
- ☐ _____
- ☐ _____

OTHER

- ☐ _____
- ☐ _____
- ☐ _____
- ☐ _____
- ☐ _____
- ☐ _____
- ☐ _____
- ☐ _____
- ☐ _____

FAMILY CAMPING

Checklist

IMPORTANT GEAR

- [ ] _____
- [ ] _____
- [ ] _____
- [ ] _____
- [ ] _____
- [ ] _____
- [ ] _____
- [ ] _____
- [ ] _____
- [ ] _____

FOOD SUPPLIES

- [ ] _____
- [ ] _____
- [ ] _____
- [ ] _____
- [ ] _____
- [ ] _____
- [ ] _____
- [ ] _____
- [ ] _____
- [ ] _____

CLOTHING

- [ ] _____
- [ ] _____
- [ ] _____
- [ ] _____
- [ ] _____
- [ ] _____
- [ ] _____
- [ ] _____
- [ ] _____
- [ ] _____

TOOLS & SUPPLIES

- [ ] _____
- [ ] _____
- [ ] _____
- [ ] _____
- [ ] _____
- [ ] _____
- [ ] _____
- [ ] _____
- [ ] _____
- [ ] _____

MISC ITEMS

- [ ] _____
- [ ] _____
- [ ] _____
- [ ] _____
- [ ] _____
- [ ] _____
- [ ] _____
- [ ] _____
- [ ] _____
- [ ] _____

OTHER

- [ ] _____
- [ ] _____
- [ ] _____
- [ ] _____
- [ ] _____
- [ ] _____
- [ ] _____
- [ ] _____
- [ ] _____
- [ ] _____

CAMPING SUPPLIES

- [ ] _____
- [ ] _____
- [ ] _____
- [ ] _____
- [ ] _____
- [ ] _____
- [ ] _____
- [ ] _____
- [ ] _____
- [ ] _____
- [ ] _____
- [ ] _____
- [ ] _____
- [ ] _____
- [ ] _____
- [ ] _____
- [ ] _____
- [ ] _____
- [ ] _____
- [ ] _____
- [ ] _____
- [ ] _____
- [ ] _____

- [ ] _____
- [ ] _____
- [ ] _____
- [ ] _____
- [ ] _____
- [ ] _____
- [ ] _____
- [ ] _____
- [ ] _____
- [ ] _____
- [ ] _____
- [ ] _____
- [ ] _____
- [ ] _____
- [ ] _____
- [ ] _____
- [ ] _____
- [ ] _____
- [ ] _____
- [ ] _____
- [ ] _____
- [ ] _____
- [ ] _____

- [ ] _____
- [ ] _____
- [ ] _____
- [ ] _____
- [ ] _____
- [ ] _____
- [ ] _____
- [ ] _____
- [ ] _____
- [ ] _____
- [ ] _____
- [ ] _____
- [ ] _____
- [ ] _____
- [ ] _____
- [ ] _____
- [ ] _____
- [ ] _____
- [ ] _____
- [ ] _____
- [ ] _____
- [ ] _____
- [ ] _____

CAMPING *Checklist*

Shelter

- [ ] TENT / CAMPER
- [ ] SLEEPING BLANKET
- [ ] PILLOWS
- [ ] TARP / COVERING

Comfort

- [ ] SLEEPING BAGS
- [ ] SHEETS & PILLOWS
- [ ] AIR MATTRESS
- [ ] AIR PUMP

- [ ] HIKING BOOTS
- [ ] SWEATERS
- [ ] RAIN JACKET
- [ ] WARM SOCKS
- [ ] T-SHIRTS
- [ ] WARM COAT
- [ ] SUN VISOR / HAT
- [ ] BATHING SUIT
- [ ] PYJAMAS

Food

- [ ] FOOD / SUPPLIES
- [ ] CONDIMENTS
- [ ] COOKWARE/POTS
- [ ] TABLE CLOTH
- [ ] PLATES & CUPS
- [ ] UTENSILS
- [ ] PAPER TOWEL
- [ ] POT HOLDERS
- [ ] DISH SOAP
- [ ] CUTLERY

Personal

- [ ] SOAP
- [ ] SHAMPOO
- [ ] TOWELS
- [ ] TOOTHPASTE
- [ ] HAIR BRUSH
- [ ] SUNSCREEN
- [ ] DEODORANT
- [ ] HAND SANITIZER
- [ ] RAZORS

Essentials

- [ ] MEDICATION
- [ ] FIRST AID KIT
- [ ] TOILET PAPER
- [ ] LIP BALM
- [ ] TISSUES
- [ ] MIRROR
- [ ] HAIR CLIPS

Important

- [ ] BATTERIES
- [ ] CAMERA
- [ ] CHARGERS
- [ ] SUNGLASSES
- [ ] FLASHLIGHT
- [ ] BUG SPRAY
- [ ] LANTERNS
- [ ] COMPASS
- [ ] BINOCULARS
- [ ] HIKING GEAR
- [ ] BACKPACK

CAMPING *Checklist*

Entertainment

- [ ] BOARD GAMES
- [ ] CARDS
- [ ] RADIO
- [ ] SPORTS GEAR

Cleaning

- [ ] BROOM / MOP
- [ ] CLEANING SUPPLIES
- [ ] CLEANING CLOTHS
- [ ] DISH TOWELS

Misc

- [ ] COFFEE POT
- [ ] FIRE KETTLE
- [ ] COOLER & ICE
- [ ] FOLDABLE TABLE
- [ ] CAMPING CHAIRS
- [ ] LIGHTER / FUEL
- [ ] FIREWOOD
- [ ] BBQ GRLL
- [ ] GARBAGE BAGS

Shopping List

- [ ]
- [ ]
- [ ]
- [ ]
- [ ]
- [ ]
- [ ]
- [ ]
- [ ]
- [ ]
- [ ]
- [ ]
- [ ]
- [ ]
- [ ]
- [ ]
- [ ]
- [ ]
- [ ]
- [ ]
- [ ]
- [ ]

CAMPING MEAL *Planner*

MONDAY

TUESDAY

WEDNESDAY

THURSDAY

FRIDAY

SATURDAY

SUNDAY

SNACK IDEAS

CAMPING *Activities*

Monday

Tuesday

Wednesday

Thursday

Friday

Saturday

Sunday

MY CAMPING *Journal*

DATE:

WHAT I DID TODAY

HIGHLIGHT OF THE DAY

CAMPING *Memories*

DATE & CAMPSITE

WHAT WE DID

HIGHLIGHT OF THE TRIP

FISHING EXPEDITION
What I've Caught

LAKE / AREA	TYPE OF FISH	WEIGHT

FAMILY CAMPING
Adventures

CAMPGROUND

DATE

ACTIVITIES

HIGHLIGHT OF THE TRIP

FAVORITE MEMORY

HIKING CHECKLIST

CLOTHING

- [ ] HIKING BOOTS
- [ ] WOOL SOCKS
- [ ] BASE LAYERS
- [ ] SHORT SLEEVED SHIRT
- [ ] LONG SLEEVED SHIRT
- [ ] INSULATED MIDLAYER
- [ ] SUN HAT / VISOR
- [ ] BANDANA
- [ ] RAINWEAR
- [ ] WATCH

EQUIPMENT

- [ ] MAP
- [ ] COMPASS
- [ ] FLASHLIGHT
- [ ] HEAD LAMP
- [ ] LIGHTER / MATCHES
- [ ] KNIFE / MULTI-TOOL
- [ ] CELL PHONE
- [ ] POUCH
- [ ] MOLESKIN
- [ ] TREKKING POLES

FOOD & SUPPLIES

- [ ] MEALS & SNACKS
- [ ] WATER BOTTLE
- [ ] WATER TREATMENT
- [ ] COOKING POT
- [ ] COOKSTOVE/FUEL
- [ ] EATING UTENSILS
- [ ] BOWL/MUG/PLATE
- [ ] GARBAGE BAGS
- [ ] ROPE
- [ ] FOLDABLE BUCKET

CAMPING GEAR

- [ ] TENT
- [ ] SLEEPING BAG
- [ ] SLEEPING PAD
- [ ] TOILET PAPER
- [ ] BACKPACK
- [ ] DUCT TAPE
- [ ] FOLDING SAW
- [ ] POT LIFTER
- [ ] CAMP SHOES
- [ ] BEAR BANGER

MISC.

- [ ] INSECT REPELLENT
- [ ] LIP BALM
- [ ] FACE PROTECTOR
- [ ] EXTRA GLOVES
- [ ] DEODORANT
- [ ] HEADPHONES
- [ ] BATTERIES
- [ ] CHARGER
- [ ] DECK OF CARDS
- [ ] GPS

OTHER

- [ ] _____
- [ ] _____
- [ ] _____
- [ ] _____
- [ ] _____
- [ ] _____
- [ ] _____
- [ ] _____
- [ ] _____
- [ ] _____

HIKING JOURNAL

TRAIL	ELEVATION GAIN	LOSS
LOCATION		

DISTANCE	DURATION	START TIME	END TIME

TRAIL TYPE	DIFFICULTY	WEATHER

IMPORTANT TRAIL DETAILS	NOTES

TRAIL SURFACE	EXPOSURE	

CAMPING *Adventures*

COLOR IN THE DATES WHEN YOU WENT CAMPING

JANUARY						
S	M	T	W	T	F	S

FEBRUARY						
S	M	T	W	T	F	S

MARCH						
S	M	T	W	T	F	S

APRIL						
S	M	T	W	T	F	S

MAY						
S	M	T	W	T	F	S

JUNE						
S	M	T	W	T	F	S

JULY						
S	M	T	W	T	F	S

AUGUST						
S	M	T	W	T	F	S

SEPTEMBER						
S	M	T	W	T	F	S

OCTOBER						
S	M	T	W	T	F	S

NOVEMBER						
S	M	T	W	T	F	S

DECEMBER						
S	M	T	W	T	F	S

CAMPING TRACKER

Where I've Been

CAMPGROUND	LOCATION	DATE

CAMPING RESERVATION

CAMPGROUND PHONE #	RESERVATION DETAILS
CONTACT PERSON	

CAMPGROUND ADDRESS	ACTIVITIES

RESTAURANTS & AMENITIES	NOTES

SITE #	NIGHTLY RATE	CHECK IN	CHECK OUT

CAMPGROUND
Amenities

- ◯ WATER
- ◯ ELECTRIC
- ◯ SEWER
- ◯ WIFI
- ◯ CABLE TV
- ◯ PETS ALLOWED
- ◯ FIRE PIT
- ◯ SHOWERS
- ◯ TENTS PERMITTED
- ◯ VISITOR PARKING
- ◯ LAUNDRY SERVICES
- ◯ BBQ AREA
- ◯ SWIMMING
- ◯ ACCESS TO BEACH / LAKE
- ◯ BOAT LAUNCH
- ◯ FISHING
- ◯
- ◯
- ◯

- ◯ POOL
- ◯ HOT TUB
- ◯ ACTIVITY CENTER
- ◯ NATURE TRAILS / HIKING
- ◯ PLAYGROUND
- ◯ BIKING / TRAILS
- ◯ GOLF COURSE
- ◯ KIDS CENTER
- ◯ FIREWORKS
- ◯ BINGO
- ◯ VOLLEYBALL
- ◯ TENNIS COURTS
- ◯ GARBAGE DISPOSAL
- ◯ CONVENIENCE STORE
- ◯ FIREWOOD/KINDLE
- ◯ PICNIC TABLES

CAMPING *Shopping List*

FAMILY CAMPING
Checklist

IMPORTANT GEAR

- ☐ Tent
- ☐ Backpack
- ☐ Tarp
- ☐ BBQ
- ☐ Sleeping Bag
- ☐ Camping Chairs
- ☐ _____
- ☐ _____
- ☐ _____
- ☐ _____
- ☐ _____

FOOD SUPPLIES

- ☐ Meals
- ☐ Snacks
- ☐ Water & Drinks
- ☐ Cook Set / Pots &
- ☐ Utensils & Dishes
- ☐ Condiments
- ☐ _____
- ☐ _____
- ☐ _____
- ☐ _____
- ☐ _____

CLOTHING

- ☐ Gloves & Hat
- ☐ Hats / Visors
- ☐ Socks & Underwear
- ☐ T-shirts & Sweaters
- ☐ Jacket / Raincoat
- ☐ Hiking Boots
- ☐ _____
- ☐ _____
- ☐ _____
- ☐ _____
- ☐ _____

TOOLS & SUPPLIES

- ☐ Lighter & Flashlights
- ☐ Firewood & Fire Starter
- ☐ Batteries
- ☐ Knife or Multi-Tool
- ☐ Compass
- ☐ _____
- ☐ _____
- ☐ _____
- ☐ _____
- ☐ _____

MISC ITEMS

- ☐ Garbage Bags
- ☐ Sunscreen
- ☐ Bug Spray/ Repellent
- ☐ Towels
- ☐ Water Bottle
- ☐ Toilet Paper
- ☐ _____
- ☐ _____
- ☐ _____
- ☐ _____

OTHER

- ☐ _____
- ☐ _____
- ☐ _____
- ☐ _____
- ☐ _____
- ☐ _____
- ☐ _____
- ☐ _____
- ☐ _____
- ☐ _____

FAMILY CAMPING
Checklist

IMPORTANT GEAR

- [ ] _____
- [ ] _____
- [ ] _____
- [ ] _____
- [ ] _____
- [ ] _____
- [ ] _____
- [ ] _____
- [ ] _____
- [ ] _____

FOOD SUPPLIES

- [ ] _____
- [ ] _____
- [ ] _____
- [ ] _____
- [ ] _____
- [ ] _____
- [ ] _____
- [ ] _____
- [ ] _____
- [ ] _____

CLOTHING

- [ ] _____
- [ ] _____
- [ ] _____
- [ ] _____
- [ ] _____
- [ ] _____
- [ ] _____
- [ ] _____
- [ ] _____
- [ ] _____

TOOLS & SUPPLIES

- [ ] _____
- [ ] _____
- [ ] _____
- [ ] _____
- [ ] _____
- [ ] _____
- [ ] _____
- [ ] _____
- [ ] _____
- [ ] _____

MISC ITEMS

- [ ] _____
- [ ] _____
- [ ] _____
- [ ] _____
- [ ] _____
- [ ] _____
- [ ] _____
- [ ] _____
- [ ] _____
- [ ] _____

OTHER

- [ ] _____
- [ ] _____
- [ ] _____
- [ ] _____
- [ ] _____
- [ ] _____
- [ ] _____
- [ ] _____
- [ ] _____
- [ ] _____

CAMPING SUPPLIES

- [ ] _____
- [ ] _____
- [ ] _____
- [ ] _____
- [ ] _____
- [ ] _____
- [ ] _____
- [ ] _____
- [ ] _____
- [ ] _____
- [ ] _____
- [ ] _____
- [ ] _____
- [ ] _____
- [ ] _____
- [ ] _____
- [ ] _____
- [ ] _____
- [ ] _____
- [ ] _____
- [ ] _____
- [ ] _____
- [ ] _____

- [ ] _____
- [ ] _____
- [ ] _____
- [ ] _____
- [ ] _____
- [ ] _____
- [ ] _____
- [ ] _____
- [ ] _____
- [ ] _____
- [ ] _____
- [ ] _____
- [ ] _____
- [ ] _____
- [ ] _____
- [ ] _____
- [ ] _____
- [ ] _____
- [ ] _____
- [ ] _____
- [ ] _____
- [ ] _____
- [ ] _____

- [ ] _____
- [ ] _____
- [ ] _____
- [ ] _____
- [ ] _____
- [ ] _____
- [ ] _____
- [ ] _____
- [ ] _____
- [ ] _____
- [ ] _____
- [ ] _____
- [ ] _____
- [ ] _____
- [ ] _____
- [ ] _____
- [ ] _____
- [ ] _____
- [ ] _____
- [ ] _____
- [ ] _____
- [ ] _____
- [ ] _____

CAMPING *Checklist*

Shelter
- [ ] TENT / CAMPER
- [ ] SLEEPING BLANKET
- [ ] PILLOWS
- [ ] TARP / COVERING

Comport
- [ ] SLEEPING BAGS
- [ ] SHEETS & PILLOWS
- [ ] AIR MATTRESS
- [ ] AIR PUMP

(untitled)
- [ ] HIKING BOOTS
- [ ] SWEATERS
- [ ] RAIN JACKET
- [ ] WARM SOCKS
- [ ] T-SHIRTS
- [ ] WARM COAT
- [ ] SUN VISOR / HAT
- [ ] BATHING SUIT
- [ ] PYJAMAS

Food
- [ ] FOOD / SUPPLIES
- [ ] CONDIMENTS
- [ ] COOKWARE/POTS
- [ ] TABLE CLOTH
- [ ] PLATES & CUPS
- [ ] UTENSILS
- [ ] PAPER TOWEL
- [ ] POT HOLDERS
- [ ] DISH SOAP
- [ ] CUTLERY

Personal
- [ ] SOAP
- [ ] SHAMPOO
- [ ] TOWELS
- [ ] TOOTHPASTE
- [ ] HAIR BRUSH
- [ ] SUNSCREEN
- [ ] DEODORANT
- [ ] HAND SANITIZER
- [ ] RAZORS

Essentials
- [ ] MEDICATION
- [ ] FIRST AID KIT
- [ ] TOILET PAPER
- [ ] LIP BALM
- [ ] TISSUES
- [ ] MIRROR
- [ ] HAIR CLIPS

Important
- [ ] BATTERIES
- [ ] CAMERA
- [ ] CHARGERS
- [ ] SUNGLASSES
- [ ] FLASHLIGHT
- [ ] BUG SPRAY
- [ ] LANTERNS
- [ ] COMPASS
- [ ] BINOCULARS
- [ ] HIKING GEAR
- [ ] BACKPACK

CAMPING *Checklist*

Entertainment

- [ ] BOARD GAMES
- [ ] CARDS
- [ ] RADIO
- [ ] SPORTS GEAR

Cleaning

- [ ] BROOM / MOP
- [ ] CLEANING SUPPLIES
- [ ] CLEANING CLOTHS
- [ ] DISH TOWELS

Misc

- [ ] COFFEE POT
- [ ] FIRE KETTLE
- [ ] COOLER & ICE
- [ ] FOLDABLE TABLE
- [ ] CAMPING CHAIRS
- [ ] LIGHTER / FUEL
- [ ] FIREWOOD
- [ ] BBQ GRLL
- [ ] GARBAGE BAGS

Shopping List

- [ ]
- [ ]
- [ ]
- [ ]
- [ ]
- [ ]
- [ ]
- [ ]
- [ ]
- [ ]
- [ ]
- [ ]
- [ ]
- [ ]
- [ ]
- [ ]
- [ ]
- [ ]
- [ ]

CAMPING MEAL *Planner*

MONDAY

TUESDAY

WEDNESDAY

THURSDAY

FRIDAY

SATURDAY

SUNDAY

SNACK IDEAS

CAMPING *Activities*

Monday

Tuesday

Wednesday

Thursday

Friday

Saturday

Sunday

MY CAMPING *Journal*

DATE:

WHAT I DID TODAY

HIGHLIGHT OF THE DAY

CAMPING *Memories*

DATE & CAMPSITE

WHAT WE DID

HIGHLIGHT OF THE TRIP

FISHING EXPEDITION
What I've Caught

LAKE / AREA	TYPE OF FISH	WEIGHT

FAMILY CAMPING
Adventures

CAMPGROUND

DATE

ACTIVITIES

HIGHLIGHT OF THE TRIP

FAVORITE MEMORY

HIKING CHECKLIST

CLOTHING

- [ ] HIKING BOOTS
- [ ] WOOL SOCKS
- [ ] BASE LAYERS
- [ ] SHORT SLEEVED SHIRT
- [ ] LONG SLEEVED SHIRT
- [ ] INSULATED MIDLAYER
- [ ] SUN HAT / VISOR
- [ ] BANDANA
- [ ] RAINWEAR
- [ ] WATCH

EQUIPMENT

- [ ] MAP
- [ ] COMPASS
- [ ] FLASHLIGHT
- [ ] HEAD LAMP
- [ ] LIGHTER / MATCHES
- [ ] KNIFE / MULTI-TOOL
- [ ] CELL PHONE
- [ ] POUCH
- [ ] MOLESKIN
- [ ] TREKKING POLES

FOOD & SUPPLIES

- [ ] MEALS & SNACKS
- [ ] WATER BOTTLE
- [ ] WATER TREATMENT
- [ ] COOKING POT
- [ ] COOKSTOVE/FUEL
- [ ] EATING UTENSILS
- [ ] BOWL/MUG/PLATE
- [ ] GARBAGE BAGS
- [ ] ROPE
- [ ] FOLDABLE BUCKET

CAMPING GEAR

- [ ] TENT
- [ ] SLEEPING BAG
- [ ] SLEEPING PAD
- [ ] TOILET PAPER
- [ ] BACKPACK
- [ ] DUCT TAPE
- [ ] FOLDING SAW
- [ ] POT LIFTER
- [ ] CAMP SHOES
- [ ] BEAR BANGER

MISC.

- [ ] INSECT REPELLENT
- [ ] LIP BALM
- [ ] FACE PROTECTOR
- [ ] EXTRA GLOVES
- [ ] DEODORANT
- [ ] HEADPHONES
- [ ] BATTERIES
- [ ] CHARGER
- [ ] DECK OF CARDS
- [ ] GPS

OTHER

- [ ] _____
- [ ] _____
- [ ] _____
- [ ] _____
- [ ] _____
- [ ] _____
- [ ] _____
- [ ] _____
- [ ] _____
- [ ] _____

HIKING JOURNAL

TRAIL	ELEVATION GAIN	LOSS
LOCATION		

DISTANCE	DURATION	START TIME	END TIME

TRAIL TYPE	DIFFICULTY	WEATHER

IMPORTANT TRAIL DETAILS	NOTES

TRAIL SURFACE	EXPOSURE

www.ingramcontent.com/pod-product-compliance
Lightning Source LLC
Chambersburg PA
CBHW08055803O426
42336CB00019B/3236